Man Overboard

Man Overboard

A Tale of Divine Compassion

poems by

David Denny

WIPF & STOCK · Eugene, Oregon

MAN OVERBOARD
A Tale of Divine Compassion

Wipf & Stock
An Imprint of Wipf and Stock Publishers
199 W. 8th Ave., Suite 3
Eugene, OR 97401
www.wipfandstock.com

ISBN 13: 978-1-49826-902-5

Manufactured in the U.S.A.

To Randal J. Pabst—pastor, friend, jonah

Like Jonah, I find myself traveling toward
my destiny in the belly of a paradox.

—THOMAS MERTON

Contents

Acknowledgments ix
Foreword by Luci Shaw xi

Part One   Hapless Servant

Arise and Go / 3
Flight / 4
Stormspeak / 5
A Fair Question / 7
Casting Lots / 8
Man Overboard / 10

Part Two   Belly of the Beast

Summoned / 13
Swallowed Whole / 14
The Great Sea / 15
Belly of the Beast / 17
God Speaks to the Great Fish / 18
A Good Question / 19

Part Three   Sackcloth and Ashes

Arise and Go Again / 23
Oracle / 24
The Perfumer and His Wife / 25
Overthrown / 27
The Courtier's Report / 28
Turning Point / 29

Contents

PART FOUR   FOOL ON THE HILL

    Jonah's Complaint / 33
    God's Response to Jonah / 35
    The Song of the Bush and the Caterpillar / 36
    On the Great Alluvial Plain / 38
    On a Hilltop Overlooking Nineveh / 41
    Parable of the Potter / 42

Afterword / 45
About the Author / 47

Acknowledgments

Grateful acknowledgment is made to the editors of the following publications in which several of these poems first appeared, some in slightly different versions:

Dappled Things: "The Perfumer and His Wife"

Pilgrim: "Jonah's Complaint" & "God's Response to Jonah."

The Sand Hill Review: "A Fair Question," "Man Overboard," "Summoned," "Swallowed Whole," "Belly of the Beast," "A Good Question."

Time of Singing: "Stormspeak" & "Casting Lots."

The author would like to express his gratitude to the kind tutelage and inspiring instruction of Anthony J. Petrotta, PhD., Associate Professor of Old Testament, Fuller Theological Seminary.

FOREWORD

IT IS EASY TO think that we know the Jonah story. It has been told us from infancy, sometimes with skepticism as we try to understand how a grown man could survive in such perilous and incredible circumstances.

But the very vividness and outlandishness of the story prints certain unforgettable incidents in our minds—God's command, Jonah's rebellion and flight, the superstitious sailors, the great storm and the great fish, the surprising conversion of the Ninevites, Jonah's refusal to forgive and forget, the arbor vine and the hungry worm. I can still see the colored flannelgraphs from my childhood Sunday School. I told the story to my own children. The tale has entered our common culture, becoming so familiar it has turned into a kind of cliché.

A cliché is a clue to what has become less than interesting through overuse. It's a French word meaning a template or metal plate, and when spoken, the word is thought to sound like a key turning in a lock, something you hear again and again as you lock and unlock your front door. When a striking image or story becomes too familiar it becomes tired, with very little left of its original force and impact.

Has that happened with our retelling of Jonah and the Whale? Do we think we know it so well that we have exhausted its possibilities? We need to look at it again!

In a brilliant reversal, David Denny has turned the familiar on its head. He closes the gap between the natural world of Jonah with supernatural directives from heaven with his fertile dramatizations of the biblical narrative, showing God rolling his eyes at Jonah's intransigence, and Jonah's defiance in the face of divine demand. In Denny's poems the ocean speaks, the wind howls, the whale thinks of himself as a merciful haven from the storm. We watch as Jonah, finally spewed up on the far shore, awaits the next directive—and this time obeys it. Individual citizens in Nineveh city take up the story, even King Sennacharib, asking for forgiveness for himself and his people.

And then, God's great transformative mercy on the repentant Ninevites reverses the sense of doom and vengeance. They are forgiven.

But Jonah, furious, wants vengeance and once again shows his independence, confident that he knows better than God what is The Right Thing To Do to his erstwhile enemies. Even the vine and the worm each sing their tales in an antiphonal duet. Denny gives them each a unique personality and voice.

These compelling poems narrate the story with telling details, drawn from authentic biblical information and retold with great force and a healthy dollop of riotous imagination. This is a first-rate way to re-enter Scripture—to not let it lie dormant in our minds because we think we know it so well, to hear it anew, and to bring it into focus, freshening our thinking and feeling so that mentally we don't coast over crucial narratives just because they're familiar.

—Luci Shaw
Bellingham, WA

Part One

Hapless Servant

Now the word of the Lord came to Jonah . . .

Arise and Go

As he lounged beneath a fig tree, gloating
for having defended the rightful borders
against a cruel enemy, I lifted him
by the front of his cloak and spoke to him
in a manner he could not mistake:
"Jonah, my faithful son, arise and go now
to Nineveh, that great city, and cry out against it.
Their wickedness has come up before me.
Cry out against it, my dove. Arise now and go."
In this way I wiped the sanctimonious
grin from his lovely face. In such a way
I roused my snoozing servant and pointed him
eastward, toward the very border he had fought
to restore. I pointed him beyond, in the direction
of Sennacherib's fortress, from which had poured
the fierce army I had turned aside, whose arrows
I had broken, whose bows I myself had bent,
upon whom I had brought darkness and despair
at mid-day, the very city from which calamity
had lately burst forth. Poor dove, poor chosen one,
I call you into the lair of the great she-beast,
a city with holocaust in her heart
and blasphemy on her ravenous lips.

But Jonah set out to flee . . . from the presence of the Lord.

Flight

I have fled to Joppa in search of a ship.
The Lord lifted me and pointed me eastward;
I turned westward and descended to the sea—
the sea, realm of Leviathan, whose chaos
I prefer to the Lord's lopsided order.
I turn my back to him. I turn away
from the one who would demean me
by sending me to the enemy's capital.
I hereby refuse his call. I would rather
wander, like Cain, marked as an outsider
forever, than betray my people to the winged
demoness of the east, whose only desire is
to devour us. To Tarshish then—to the unholy
ends of the earth! For the Mighty One,
rather than crush our enemy with his righteous
fist, would open his hand in friendship;
he would betray us by his unbridled mercy.
As I assembled my belongings, my wife
clicked about my burning ears like a locust.
"Obey Him," she cried, "or bring down havoc
on us all." I spat on the doorpost of the house
I left behind. I put my children into the care
of the woman who is no longer my wife.
I shook the dust from my sandals. Along
the winding path to Joppa, I untied all 613 knots
in my tallit. Like this ragged piece of wool,
my life has come undone. I hereby toss it
into the roiling surf. I have fled to Joppa
in search of a ship—any ship will do.

But the Lord hurled a great wind upon the sea . . .

Stormspeak

The Lord bade me to whirl around Job,
confounding and humbling him.

The Lord instructed me to sweep past Elijah,
nearly plucking him from the cliff face.

The Lord beckoned me to lift the waters of the Red Sea
like a veil so that Moses might pass through.

Once again he has roused me to give this
new prophet a taste of chaos. He raised me up

from the sea to wrestle this little one, using
wind, rain, and waves to throw his mind out of joint.

He called me to rattle his poor dove's fragile heart
within the cage of his ribs. "Bring him to the edge

of the darkness he seeks," he said.
"Cause his ship to split and her contents to cry out.

Let these creatures hear my voice in you.
Do not be silent until my prophet has been

vomited out." The task appeared simple:
I saw the storm within him and mimicked it.

Who would have known how thick was his hide?
I rose up around Jonah, who hid in the depths

of the ship. Yes, deep in the hold his prophet
snoozed and snored. Like a baby, he curled

into slumber, protected in the ship's womb.
I pounded her with waves like battering rams.

I emptied my bladder upon the deck. I blew
until the wooden beams began to weep.

A hard breech delivery it was, but finally he
emerged—blanched, shivering, nauseous—

with the fear of the Lord in his heart
and the terror of the deep on his face.

Jonah, meanwhile, had gone down into the hold of the ship . . .

A Fair Question

After we set sail, I made my way to the deepest
part of the ship, to a dark, cave-like corner
where the grain sacks were piled. There I
nested between two sacks and drifted
into a deep sleep. As I boy I had found
such a spot in the anterooms of the great temple
in Jerusalem. My parents and older brothers
were taking Zebulun's ram to the priests.
I wandered off. The priests found me
the next morning and chased me into
the courtyard and into the arms of my
red-faced family. In my sleep I rode
an unruly camel eastward. I kept kicking him,
trying to turn him around. In the nightmare,
our caravan consisted of disfigured women,
lame children, and old men. The Lord had put me
in charge of a caravan of fools, a silly brigade
of outcast clowns bound for danger. Finally
my camel stumbled and I was thrown to the sand.
I awoke in the hull of the little ship with water
all around. I vomited the barley loaf I had eaten
in Joppa. I stumbled to the ladder. On deck
I struggled to keep my balance as the ship
pitched and rolled. A storm like no other raged
against us. The captain and his small crew
bowed before three idols. The captain grabbed me
by the arm and pulled me to my knees.
"Who is your god?" he cried over the howling wind.

The sailors said to one another, "Come, let us cast lots, so that we may know on whose account this calamity has come upon us."

Casting Lots

Right away we could see that this storm
was different from all others: it swooped
down on us like a hawk. The captain tried
to hide his fear, but when he ordered us
to toss the cargo overboard, our own fears
were confirmed: if we didn't work fast, we
were doomed. We had our three most powerful
idols on deck, and had begun our supplication,
when up from the innards of the ship came
the shivering little man who had so hastily
bought passage in Joppa, his cloak covered
with his vomit. The captain produced
the pot shards; we each scratched our mark.
He cast them on the heaving deck and read them
through the driving raindrops. Three times
the lot fell upon the stranger. Who was he
and which god had he offended? Sick of his
timid answers, the captain smacked him across
the face and cried, "What have you done?"
"Throw me into the sea," the man replied.
What a curse he was, this little Hebrew:
if he stayed on board, we would perish; if we
threw an innocent man overboard, we would perish.
The captain had little time to consider.
The waves smacked us to the breaking point.
We could barely hear him over the din of
the great storm, but we think our captain yelled,
"Throw him back into the arms of the god he flees!"
We scooped him up and hurled him as we had
the sacks and crates and bottles. He never did
bob to the surface. Almost immediately the rain
turned to mist, the wind ceased, and the waves
receded. We tossed our idols overboard.

We got on our knees and gave thanks to the god
who had saved us, the god whose lot had
fallen three times upon his hapless servant.

So they picked Jonah up and threw him into the sea . . .

Man Overboard

As a boy I had a vivid dream in which I was a bird,
flying effortlessly over our neighbor's vineyard.
Seeing that his grapes were ripe, I glided down
among the vines and perched atop an arbor, eating
my fill of the sweet, delicious fruit. Suddenly
our neighbor's dog bounded into the vineyard,
barking insanely, foaming at the mouth.
My bird's belly too full to fly away, I sat atop
my perch and watched him come for me.
I awoke in a sweat, the last thought in my avian mind
that in only a few steps I would be devoured.
I recalled that dream the moment the sailors
hoisted me into their arms and sent me flying
over the bow of their little ship. One moment
I was completely free; the next I was sinking fast
in a gray-green froth, completely at the mercy
of that rabid beast my teachers had identified
as the Great Sea. Having drawn my last breath,
I sank into the depths, this prayer foremost in my mind:
"For your sake we are slain all day long, and accounted
as sheep for the slaughter." Swirling around me
were grain sacks and bottles. One of the huge idols
I had seen on deck sank beside me, its bejeweled eyes
staring blankly into mine. As I sank downward,
up from the depths arose a giant shadow. Is it you,
O Lord? And then darkness overtook me.
The only sound the beating of my own feeble heart.

Part Two

BELLY OF THE BEAST

But the Lord provided a large fish to swallow up Jonah . . .

Summoned

Long have I swum in the cold darkness,
among the canyons of the deep, waiting.
Since the day of my fashioning I lived
in his bounty, growing, playing; he
nourished me with manna of the sea;
he sheltered and nurtured me, taught me
how to be. Then today this new sensation:
his power surging through my bones
and sinews. He called me into ascent—
joyfully, with my whole heart did I respond,
turning and turning in an upward gyre toward
the warm light. At last all has become clear:
for this was I made. Now I know why
my jaws gape so. Now I know why my belly
is hollow like a small cave and will not
digest flesh. Up from the fathoms I arose
until his prophet floundered before me
among the jetsam. I opened wide and felt
the little one settle into the place next
to my heart. After his tight body loosened,
I caught a glimpse of the vessel and her crew,
worshipping the one who so fearfully and
wonderfully made me. And now the steady,
smooth descent, the sleeping one locked within.
Reversing the gyre, I return now to the cold
canyons of the deep, waiting to be called again.

. . . and Jonah was in the belly of the fish for three days and three nights.

Swallowed Whole

Not a speck of light shines
into my cramped prison cell;
the darkness is so thick
I have forgotten what light was like.

At first my legs hurt, tucked
up beneath my beard. Now
they have gone numb; I embrace
them with my useless arms.

I feel myself drifting like a feather,
sinking like a millstone.
My hair is wrapped in weeds,
my feet tangled among roots.

I hear only the sound of a great
heartbeat. Is it you, O Lord?
Is that you here beside me
in the dark? Forsake me not!

Have mercy on your servant, Lord;
rescue me from my despair.
Shower me once again with loving-kindness;
pull me out from this deep pit.

You cast me into the deep, / into the heart of the seas, / and the flood surrounded me; / all your waves and your billows / passed over me.

The Great Sea

You love me; you fear me.
You call me great, and so I am.
For I can carry you
where you don't want to go.

I can wrap you in seaweed
and drag you by the hair.
I can take you down to
where the cavefish dwell.

I can churn you like butter
in an ever-spinning wheel.
I can plump you in my brine,
shine you like a well-turned stone.

You fear me; you love me.
You call me great, and so I am.
For though I am wild,
yet I can be tamed.

I cool you with my breezes.
I soothe you with my waves.
I feed you from my bounty.
I move you on my tides.

In me you dangle your children's feet.
You swim along my sandy shores.
On moonlit nights you sing to me.
You gaze upon me from afar.

You love me; you fear me.
You call me great, and so I am.
For now I hold you to my bosom,
now I fling you wide upon the earth.

Then I said, "I am driven away / from your sight; / how shall I look again / upon your holy temple?"

Belly of the Beast

In a vision I see the terraces where
my fig trees grow, my barley fields below;
my neighbor's vineyard lies farther on,
in the valley beneath my home.

Will I ever see my wife again,
washing her hair among the reeds
in the shallows of the Jordan?
Will I look upon her face in lamplight?

Will I ever hear the chirping
of my children's voices again?
Will I hear their joyful yelps
among the spring lambs and goats?

Will I ever again ascend Mount Zion,
hear the singing in the temple courtyard,
smell the sweet smoke rising
from the burnt offerings?

Have mercy on your servant, Lord;
rescue me from my despair.
Shower me once again with loving-kindness;
pull me out from this deep pit.

Then the Lord spoke to the fish . . .

God Speaks to the Great Fish

To you, my lovely, the gates of deep darkness
have been revealed. Your eyes, my sweet,
flash forth light, and your eyelids hide
the dawn. You, my languorous one,
make the deep swirl like a boiling pot,
and you, oh my lovely, sweet, and languorous
one, turn the very sea into a roiling cauldron.
Rise up now, great one, and free the captive
in your belly. Release him so that he may know
my loving-kindness toward him and all creation.
Show him how power is made the servant of love,
how death is now but a fallen city, a smoldering
ruin. Arise and go to the eastern shore. Set him
afoot again upon the dry land, the memory
of you aflame in his rebel mind, my mercy
the only moisture upon his parched lips.

. . . and it spewed Jonah out upon the dry land.

A Good Question

Awake and yet in slumber, I drifted in the darkness.
I wept for all that was lost and prayed to be restored
to life. I don't know how long I lay confined.
The great hand that held me in its palm now began
to squeeze me in its grip. I began to slip and turn
within the walls of my chamber. Soon I was covered
in a kind of mucous. Then came a sound like
a rushing wind. My ears filled with it until I was deaf.
The squeezing in my chamber grew rapid until
suddenly I was shot through a narrow canal.
My ears broke open; I heard a great roar.
I was thrust into blinding light and vomited upon
the sand. I dragged myself toward some rocks and
nested between two large boulders, hiding from the sun.
There I lay in limbo until the air cooled, the moon shown
above my head, and hunger pangs dug at my ribs.
Pulled upright, I saw myself in the jagged moonlight:
a poor, bedraggled creature coughed up from the deep,
covered in slime and sand and blood and dung.
The voice of the one who was once called Jonah rose up
within me. I heard him ask, "Can a man be born twice?"

Part Three

SACKCLOTH AND ASHES

The word of the Lord came to Jonah a second time . . .

Arise and Go Again

Seeing the dry bones of
my chosen ones scattered
on the ground, I am he who
raises up, who clothes them
in sinews and flesh, who
wraps them in new skin;
I am he who breathes life
into the lifeless, who brings
hope to those in despair.
Humbled now, my dove was
prepared to listen and obey.
I gave him food and drink.
For three days I nourished him.
I spoke to his softened heart:
"Arise, go to Nineveh, that great city,
and proclaim to it the message
that I tell you." Eastward
he walked. Along the way,
he gathered unto himself
again the desire to speak and
sing and sit in the company
of humans and other animals.
He walked across the desert
in my service, standing at last
before the gate of the great
she-beast, vulnerable to her
immense fangs and sharp talons.
The only armor covering his
reluctant heart, my message.
I am the God who breathes life
into dust. I will show mercy
on whom I will show mercy.

So Jonah set out and went to Nineveh, according to the word of the Lord.

Oracle

I walked right into the center of the great plaza.
They gave me a wooden platform to stand on.

I let them have it, this message of doom.
And why not? I had been swallowed by

a great fish and held for three days in Sheol.
When you've been dead, what else can they do?

"Yet forty days, and Nineveh shall be overthrown!"
Imagine me saying this in Jerusalem.

They would toss me into Kidron's ditch
and leave me for the vultures. But here,

in the enemy's bosom, they opened their arms,
every one of them: servants, merchants, priests,

even the king himself, who tossed aside his
crown, bowed upon his marble floor,

and pasted himself with tears and ashes.
Every one of them tore his robes in grief.

Every one of them stopped eating and drinking.
These pagans have put us to shame,

embracing him the way a bride, after
long betrothal, finally receives her beloved.

And the people of Nineveh believed God; they proclaimed a fast, and everyone, great and small, put on sackcloth.

The Perfumer and His Wife

The prophets of Ashur and Ishtar are shaven smooth
and heavily perfumed. They go about in white robes
with golden stoles of silk. We pay a fine for crossing
their path too narrowly. Even the temple prostitutes
keep their distance. This little foreigner entered with
the animals by the Mashki Gate, looking every bit as
ragged and matted as the weary cattle, goats, and sheep who
accompanied him. At first we mistook him for yet another
beggar in the marketplace. Then he announced himself
as a prophet of the Lord. Thieves and muggers began to
circle him; he took no notice. When he spoke, it was not
with the measured stentorian tones of our own scribes;
it was more like the growl of one of Ishtar's bronze lions
come to life. He was strange and pitiful, yet somehow
he commanded authority, even among the many
competing noises of the afternoon trade. He took a stand
in the shade of Sennacherib's palace without rival.
We felt sorry for him because he claimed to serve only
one god. My first impulse was to offer him some of our own
household gods; we have so many, we cannot appease
them all. But then he spoke of the attributes and
the achievements of his lone god; we remembered
the tale of Sodom and Gomorrah and our hearts grew
heavy with dread. Something was deeply wrong
in Nineveh, and we had grown weary of the official
explanations. Harsh though his words were, we heard
in them the truth we had tacitly feared: our violence
and our indolence, our bile and our enmity—the vomit
we had collectively returned to—had begun to poison
all within our city walls. I have never been prouder
of my wife when she closed our booth early for the day
and guided him—*Dove*, he called himself—to the river
where she bathed and fed him. And when he told us

that like a fox without a den he had nowhere to lay
his head, we took him home and sheltered him for the night.

When the news reached the king of Nineveh, he rose from his throne, removed his robe, covered himself with sackcloth, and sat in ashes.

Overthrown

Nineveh had developed an appetite that could never
be satisfied. The more meat we devoured, the greater
our hunger pangs. From without, we seemed a champion
that could never be vanquished. From within, we felt
ourselves a sickened beast, still clear-eyed and muscled,
but with maggots multiplying in our bowels.

Once the cause of jubilation in the streets, the return
of our triumphant armies were now greeted with apathy.
The great temple of Ishtar, mighty patroness of our cause,
became a house of empty rituals. Even my palace—
a palace without rival on this earth—appeared to all who
walked its corridors merely a compound of shadow and echo.

Atop it all, plague swooped into the city every autumn
like a vulture, snatching up the best right along with
the worst. Though our priests and prophets denied it
to my face, behind my back they admitted that our blessing
had turned curse; it was only a matter of time until
our enemies tasted the sour water of the once-sweet Tigris.

The words of the little Hebrew hit us like a fierce sirocco.
Scrolls in my library told of his god's anger against pharaoh.
My mind reeled through the night with images of locusts
and blood, hail and darkness. And so in the morning I
sent forth my decree. "Who knows?" I said to any who
were still listening. "Perhaps this god will yet show mercy."

Then he had a proclamation made in Nineveh . . . No human being or animal, no herd or flock, shall taste anything. They shall not feed, nor shall they drink water. Human beings and animals shall be covered with sackcloth, and they shall cry mightily to God.

The Courtier's Report

Hearing that his people and the animals
had heeded the prophet's warning,
Sennacherib arose and left his throne
and came down into the courtyard,
dropping his robes piece by piece
as he walked. He sat on a heap of ashes,
a cloak of sackcloth was wrapped
obediently around his shoulders.
There he sat, refusing food and water,
muttering a litany beneath his breath
over and over to the gnats and
the mosquitoes who buzzed
around his crownless head.
And after three days and nights
he stood and walked the streets
of Nineveh, from his palace to the banks
of the Tigris, through the gardens
and along the canals, around the temples
and atop the aquaduct he had built.
Everywhere the people of Nineveh
sat in sackcloth and ashes, seeking
the favor of Jonah's god. And their
king for the first time walked among them.

When God saw what they did, how they turned from their evil ways,
God changed his mind about the calamity that he had said he would
bring upon them . . .

Turning Point

You have heard my prophet and changed your course.
I have heard your cries, as a father hears his ailing child
call to him in the night. I arise and go to you. Fear not,
for I hereby withhold my anger. I restrain myself.

You have turned towards me and I now turn towards you,
as dancers reach for one another and twirl in their delight.
You have let go of Ishtar's rage and clung to my compassion.
The arm I once raised against you I now extend to you

in friendship. I receive you as my own. I embrace you
as my child, for you have cried to me in true repentance.
I too repent, for when your heart softened, so my heart also
softened, and when you turned from your wickedness,

I turned to you in loving-kindness and extend to you the same
mercy I extend to my beloved, my dove, my chosen one.
My heart delights in you, for you were lost and now
you are found; though you were dead, yet shall you live.

Part Four

FOOL ON THE HILL

But this was very displeasing to Jonah, and he became angry.

Jonah's Complaint

I set up camp east of Nineveh
on a hill overlooking the great city.
There I waited for fire and smoke.
I waited for an army to lay siege,
for an earthquake to lay flat
the walls, or a plague to empty
the streets and markets and temples.
Nothing happened. Not one thing.
And so I am a false prophet.

Why, O Lord, have you hauled me
through the guts of a great fish,
spat me back out and nursed me,
strengthened me to deliver
your final warning?—and then
nothing. Not even a mild breeze
has been lifted against our enemy.
You have opened your fist and held
up your palm as one who surrenders.

Answer me: Should evil go unpunished?
I was your obedient prophet of doom!
You raised me up to foretell your fury:
Nineveh, that open, festering sore,
that stinking pit of rotting meat,
haven of thieves and slave-traders,
sanctuary to those who flaunt your laws—
Nineveh, womb of terror and violence,
forger of spears that pierce your heart.

For generations Israel has sung
your praises, loved your statutes,
worn your word upon our foreheads
and forearms, sacrificed firstfruits,

consecrated its children to you.
Is this how you reward us—with mercy
as cheap as the harlot in the window?
For this reason I turned my back to you.
For this reason I set my sights on Tarshish.

As I was once swallowed by death,
I now find myself consumed by anger.
I would rather die than return to Israel.
You should have left me to rot
in the belly of Sheol, my hair wrapped
in weeds, my feet tangled among roots.
Any old fool could have spoken
your hollow cry of judgment.
It's plain to see that any old fool did.

Beneath me now, in the great city
on the plain, I hear the happy noises
of a thanksgiving banquet. They feast
upon fatted calves and toast their salvation.
I should have known that the Lord
was merciful above all, slow to anger,
likely to repent, that his loving-kindness,
like the wings of a great bird,
covers the wicked as well as the good.

But God said to Jonah, "Is it right for you to be angry . . . ?"

God's Response to Jonah

I watched you stalk from the city and perch
yourself upon that lonely hill to the east; like Cain,
you must decide whether your anger will
drive you to my bosom or to Nod, to Tarshish.
I see you digging your heels into the soil,
blood rising in your cheeks and forehead.
That hasty shelter you have fashioned, my dove,
will not shade you well enough, for
the real heat of the day comes from within.

Is it right for you to burn this way? To snort and
stamp like the bulls of Bashan? Where were you
when the Tigris began to flow? Where were you
when the walls of Nineveh were hoisted toward the sky?
And where were you when Sennacherib's father
taught him to pull crocodiles from the bulrushes,
to stalk gazelles with only a bow and arrow?
Do you not know that the judgment you wish
for others may just as well fall upon yourself?

I am the God who breathes life into dust.
I accompanied my people through forty years
in the wilderness of Sinai. I chose David
to be king in an everlasting covenant.
I brought you through three days and nights
in the belly of Sheol so that you might
bear the message that saved 120,000
who didn't know their left hand from their right.
I will have mercy upon whom I will have mercy.

The Lord God appointed a bush, and made it come up over Jonah . . .
God appointed a worm that attacked the bush, so that it withered.

Song of the Bush and the Caterpillar

I am the bush
called to grow in the night
while the prophet sleeps.

> I am the caterpillar
> appointed to eat the bush
> that grows in the night
> while the prophet sleeps.

Through my green fuse
runs the spark of life.

> I bring blight and death
> to every green thing.

My vines stretch,
my leaves unfurl,
and I grow.

> My jaws devour leaf
> and vine, and I grow.

My shade will soothe
the prophet's anger.

> My appetite is never-ending.
> My task is never finished.

The prophet will find
shelter in my shade.

The prophet will lie
exposed to heat, wind, sun.

Through me the Lord
gives and gives.
Blessed be His name.

Through me the Lord
takes and takes away.
Blessed be His name.

"And should I not be concerned about Nineveh, that great city, in which there are more than a hundred and twenty thousand people . . . and also many animals?"

On the Great Alluvial Plain

Cattle

The chewing of cud is an endless obsession.

This time of year the body slows,
the moon rises earlier than usual,
and you wonder how much longer you have.

The flies gather in your eyes;
you don't even bother to
flick your tail to disturb them.

You just want your utter emptied
so you can lie under a tree and
let the calves do all the lowing.

You remember being a calf once
but the ache in your hips and neck
remind you that it was long ago.

When they swing the final gate shut
behind you, you might even
be glad to give the field over to the young.

There is a certain sound that arises
from the barn on such afternoons.
A kind of cry that reminds you of birthing

only sharper and higher and shorter
than the long, slow moans of labor.
We lift our heads for a moment

and then continue chewing our cud.

Goats

There is a foreboding stir among us—
as though a storm were on the rise,
and yet the sky is free of darkness.
The air is charged as when we climb
to the high pasture—yet we stand together
on the great plain, the ground seeming
to shift beneath our hooves. We rub
against each other for reassurance.
The young males jostle to be at the center
of the flock; the elder females circle.
Our shepherds have ceased their shouts
and whistles; they stand apart from us,
gazing up into the eastern sky.
Do they also sense that somewhere
in the distance a knife is being drawn
across a sharpening stone?

Sheep

We are heavy with wool. Any day now
we will be wrestled to the ground
and sheared by our shepherd's burly sons.

Not long now until we're herded bleating
and leaping through the Mashki Gate,
our whole lives a prelude to this last parade.

What prompts us to move in tandem
across the great plain like the tide,
our dogs barking and the rod poking

at our sides? Goats cry in the distance.
We know we are made for slaughter,
and yet over us this afternoon breaks

a wave of peace and contentment
as if we have all been spared the knife.
Instead we feel the reassuring tap

of our shepherd's staff, the anointing
of our daily wounds with oil, a water trough,
and the easing towards evening routine.

*. . . and the sun beat down on the head of Jonah so that he was faint
and asked that he might die.*

On a Hilltop Overlooking Nineveh

I can't go back home.
My stomach can't hold
that much crow: the smug
expression on my wife's face,
the jeers of the Levites
in the temple courtyard,
the questions and later
the embarrassed silence
of my children.

I could stay here,
in Nineveh. The perfumer
said he would build me
a house near his own.
His wife would cook
for me. I could tend
his garden and bathe
in the murky Tigris.
What is a prophet anyway?

A prophet is someone
who answers a call.
Often his hand is forced;
he dreams of another life
because this one is wrecked.
That's all I now know.
I would like to watch the sunset
from another angle. Tarshish is nice,
I hear, in springtime . . . .

Then the Lord said, "You are concerned about the bush, for which you did not labor and which you did not grow . . . And should I not be concerned about Nineveh . . . ?"

Parable of the Potter

I am who I am,
not who you have
fashioned me to be
in your selfish thoughts.

Does not the potter
maintain the right
to create as he sees fit,
to make or destroy?

I have shaped a dove
from a lump of wet clay,
dried him in the sun,
then taught him to fly.

Now the dove returns
to the potter and
tells him he was wrong
to give him flight.

Because he despises
the potter's other creations,
he prefers to be dashed
against the rocks.

Who knows the mind
of the potter?
Who can fathom
his intentions?

I am the Lord, your God,
gracious and merciful,
slow to anger,
abounding in steadfast love.

AFTERWORD

THE CAST OF CHARACTERS in this biblical folktale is as far-ranging and inclusive as one of Walt Whitman's famous catalogues. It includes practically every strata of ancient society: sailors and shepherds, merchants and priests, even the powerful king of a notorious empire. Boldly, the author gives special emphasis to herd animals, a giant sea creature, an assortment of "natural" phenomena, even a hungry caterpillar and a miraculous night-growing vine. The tale of Jonah is crawling with life forms, all of them under the loving care of a gracious creator.

But the focus of our attention is Jonah himself, an odd, irascible sort of anti-hero, who satirizes the role of prophet even as he grudgingly fulfills its requirements. At first glance, he appears to be a coward. Then he hops aboard a cargo ship full of salty pagans bound for the ends of the earth, an act requiring tremendous courage. In a Mark Twain meets James Bond moment, he emerges from the womb-like tomb inside the belly of the great fish and treks across the desert, resembling the animals who accompany him through the slaughter gate of the metropolis. Like Buster Keaton, the universe seems aligned against him, but somehow we know he will come out all right in the end.

And he sort of does. After the extreme success of what must be the most concise evangelical sermon in history, Jonah, rather than celebrating victory, succumbs to a pity party on a nearby hillside. Many readers are puzzled by his reaction. Jonah, it seems, cannot be pleased with his own success. Rabbinical commentators supply a possible motivation: there was no worse reputation in Israelite society than that of false prophet. Having foretold the Ninevites' doom in such a public way, their repentance and God's mercy must feel to Jonah like the ultimate betrayal.

For his part, God is nothing if not mysterious and unpredictable. This tale illustrates the old adage that his ways are certainly not our ways. For the Ninevites, that is a very good thing. And so it is for Jonah, though his ego is too badly bruised for him to consider himself as an object lesson in the radical nature of God's justice. Ultimately, Jonah's predicament is ours:

the dramatic tension between Jonah and God echoes our own complicated relationship with the divine conspiracy of mercy in our world. About this, the biblical author speaks to us across time and culture, landscape and language.

Are we any less fragile than poor Jonah as we stumble through our own post-modern Ninevehs? As with any effective satire, the object of the story's ridicule is us—that is, the Jonah within us all. Addled by our own brand of anger and fear, how often do we run from the opportunities God puts before us to act as agents of his love in hostile territory? Distracted by our media-saturated culture, numb to the victims of our empirical ambitions, weary of the hard-spun official proclamations—well, it's enough to send us shopping on the internet for cheap fares to Tarshish. And when we're finished whining, pouting, and swearing, the open question at the end of Jonah's tale is also directed at us: given that we serve at the pleasure of a God who is slow to anger, rich in mercy, and abounding in steadfast love, how then should we live?

—David Denny
Cupertino, CA

About the Author

David Denny is the author of *Fool in the Attic* (Aldrich Press, 2013) and *Plebeian on the Front Porch* (Finishing Line Press, 2012). His poems and short stories have appeared in numerous literary journals, including *Atlanta Review*, *California Quarterly*, *Iodine Poetry Journal*, *Pearl*, and *The Sun*. He holds an MFA in creative writing from the University of Oregon and an MAT degree from Fuller Theological Seminary. Denny is Professor of English at De Anza College and former editor of *Bottomfish* magazine. He is the recipient of a 2013 Artist Laureate award by the Arts Council of Silicon Valley, and he recently completed a two-year term as inaugural Poet Laureate of Cupertino, California.

www.ingramcontent.com/pod-product-compliance
Lightning Source LLC
Chambersburg PA
CBHW070830100426
42813CB00003B/564